W9-BRA-862

J 363.122
M00

EMERGENCY RESPONSE

CHILDREN'S LIBRARY

FEMA

PREPARE, RESPOND, AND RECOVER

Carla Mooney

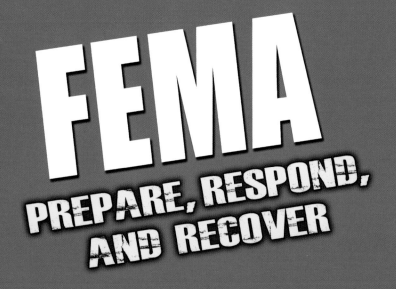

Rourke
Educational Media
rourkeeducationalmedia.com

Scan for Related Titles and
Teacher Resources

Before Reading:

Building Academic Vocabulary and Background Knowledge

Before reading a book, it is important to tap into what your child or students already know about the topic. This will help them develop their vocabulary, increase their reading comprehension, and make connections across the curriculum.

1. Look at the cover of the book. What will this book be about?
2. What do you already know about the topic?
3. Let's study the Table of Contents. What will you learn about in the book's chapters?
4. What would you like to learn about this topic? Do you think you might learn about it from this book? Why or why not?
5. Use a reading journal to write about your knowledge of this topic. Record what you already know about the topic and what you hope to learn about the topic.
6. Read the book.
7. In your reading journal, record what you learned about the topic and your response to the book.
8. After reading the book complete the activities below.

Content Area Vocabulary

Read the list. What do these words mean?

agency
assess
civil defense
communications systems
coordinated
counseling
debris
evacuated
federal
first responders
floodplains
infrastructure
mitigation
oversees
property
simulating
toxic

After Reading:

Comprehension and Extension Activity

After reading the book, work on the following questions with your child or students in order to check their level of reading comprehension and content mastery.

1. If FEMA is the agency that helps when disasters strike, then why should citizens attend trainings provided by FEMA? (Inferring)
2. If FEMA was no longer an agency, what would happen to towns and cities after disasters? (Asking questions)
3. Why is it important to know the climate and weather patterns of where you live? (Text to self connection)
4. What is FEMA's role during a disaster? (Summarize)
5. Describe how FEMA helps people prepare for a disaster. (Summarize)

Extension Activity

Think about your community. Do you live where a tornado or hurricane can happen? Are you close to a nuclear plant or a river that can flood? How can you help people prepare for a disaster? Create a poster that provides members of your community with key information that will help them when a disaster strikes.

TABLE OF CONTENTS

If a hurricane destroys your community, where can you turn for help? The Federal Emergency Management **Agency** (FEMA) will help you. Every year, disasters strike the United States. Some disasters occur naturally, such as a hurricane or an earthquake. Other disasters are man-made, such as a chemical spill or a nuclear reactor leak. In any disaster, FEMA is ready to help people survive and recover.

EMERGENCY FACT
In 2011, there were nearly 200 weather-related events in the United States that caused at least $1 billion in damage.

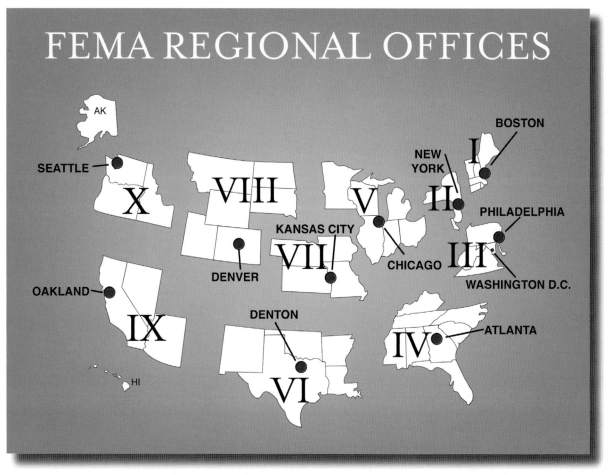

FEMA REGIONAL OFFICES

AK

BOSTON

NEW YORK

SEATTLE

X

VIII

V

II

PHILADELPHIA

KANSAS CITY

CHICAGO

III

WASHINGTON D.C.

DENVER

VII

OAKLAND

IX

DENTON

IV

ATLANTA

HI

VI

There are 10 regional FEMA offices located across the country. Each office responds to emergencies in their area.

When a disaster strikes, local and state officials respond first. If they need help, the **federal** government steps in to assist. FEMA **oversees** the federal government's response to a disaster. The agency's employees help people get things they need, such as food, clean water, and a place to sleep. FEMA workers transport injured people to hospitals. They set up **communications systems** so people can get important information.

Mobile Communications
Office Vehicle (MCOV)

After a disaster, FEMA helps people recover. It helps people find temporary housing. People who have missing family, friends, and pets can get help finding them. FEMA offers low-interest loans and grants of money to rebuild. FEMA also provides **counseling** to survivors.

After a disaster, families may write notes on their destroyed homes about missing people or pets.

FEMA wants communities to be prepared should a disaster strike. FEMA offers training for citizens on what to do in an emergency. It helps community leaders plan for disasters. It also holds training sessions at FEMA's National Emergency Training Center for **first responders**, such as police, firefighters, and emergency medical workers. **Simulating** a disaster can help communities prepare for a real disaster when it occurs.

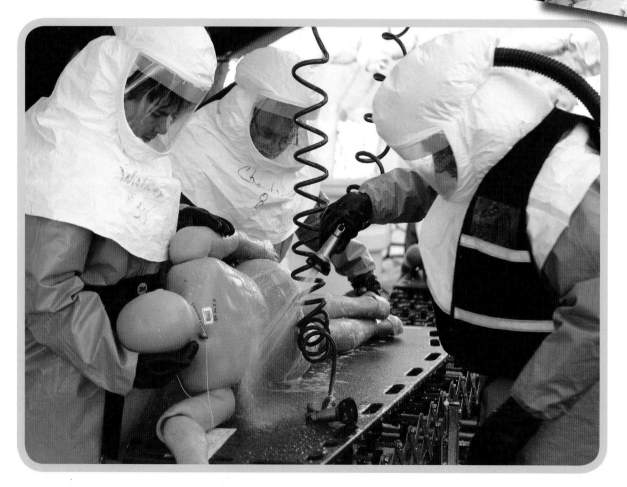

First responders practice decontaminating a simulated disaster survivor.

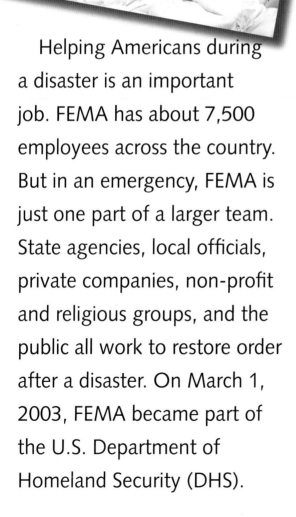

Helping Americans during a disaster is an important job. FEMA has about 7,500 employees across the country. But in an emergency, FEMA is just one part of a larger team. State agencies, local officials, private companies, non-profit and religious groups, and the public all work to restore order after a disaster. On March 1, 2003, FEMA became part of the U.S. Department of Homeland Security (DHS).

Department of Homeland Security (DHS)

The DHS's mission is to protect the United States from threats. It is made up of 22 different federal departments and agencies, including FEMA. The department works to prevent terrorism against the United States, secure borders, prepare for disasters, and protect the country's computer information systems.

The federal government oversees the whole of the United States. But it has a long history of helping communities when a disaster strikes. In 1803, the government helped a New Hampshire town after a large fire. In the following years, Congress passed legislation to help people after hurricanes, earthquakes, floods, and other natural disasters.

In the 1930s, the federal government paid for buildings, roads, and bridges to be repaired after natural disasters.

New England Hurricane of 1938

Miami, Florida September, 1945

Florida Hurricane of 1947

It also paid for the building of levees, floodwalls, and pumps to protect communities from floods. The government also started responding to disasters to reduce injury and damage.

In the 1960s and 1970s, many large natural disasters hit the United States. In 1961, Hurricane Carla devastated the Texas coast. The Alaskan Earthquake of 1964 killed 131 people and damaged many homes and buildings. In 1971, the San Fernando Earthquake shook Southern California. In each of these disasters, many agencies handled emergency services. Some were part of the federal government. Others were part of state or local governments. It was confusing to know who was in charge.

Alaska Earthquake, 1964

To make responding to a disaster easier, Congress passed a new law called the Disaster Relief Act. If a disaster is small, it can be handled by local and state agencies. Sometimes, a disaster is so big that communities need federal help and money. When a president declares a disaster, the federal government can fund emergency relief and damage repair.

President Jimmy Carter
(1924-)

In 1979, President Jimmy Carter created FEMA. The new agency was responsible for coordinating the federal government's response to a disaster. FEMA also took over **civil defense**.

EMERGENCY FACT
President Barack Obama has declared a record-breaking 99 disasters.

Since its formation, FEMA helped people in many natural disasters. It responded to 1989's Loma Prieta Earthquake, 1992's Hurricane Andrew, and 2012's Hurricane Sandy. FEMA also responded to nuclear and chemical emergencies.

Hurricane Sandy damages Casino Pier in Seaside Heights, New Jersey.

In 1978, FEMA responded to a **toxic** chemical spill at Love Canal in New York. It also organized the response to the nuclear accident at Pennsylvania's Three Mile Island nuclear power plant.

Three Mile Island experiences a partial nuclear meltdown in 1979.

In March 2003, FEMA became part of the newly formed Department of Homeland Security. The department was formed after the terrorist attacks on September 11, 2001. The department's mission is to protect the United States from the many threats it faces every day, both natural and man-made.

Responding to a disaster does not always go as planned. In 2005, Hurricane Katrina devastated New Orleans. Many people were stranded and unable to find the help they needed. FEMA was harshly criticized for its poor response.

After Hurricane Sandy, a home is elevated to protect against future flooding.

Preparing for a disaster can save lives and **property**. In addition to training communities for disaster response, FEMA helps communities understand disaster risks and plan **mitigation** activities. Mitigation activities are designed to prevent a disaster from having a devastating impact. For example, FEMA works with architects to design buildings that can withstand earthquakes and hurricanes.

Being prepared can make a big difference in getting through a disaster. That is why FEMA instructs homeowners on how to protect their homes from fires, floods, and other disasters.

Through the National Flood Insurance Program, FEMA makes sure that homeowners in **floodplains** can get affordable flood insurance. It also helps people move buildings located on floodplains to prevent future loss.

During the Flood of 2006, Lourdes Hospital in Binghamton, New York **evacuated** patients and shut down operations. The hospital is located on a floodplain on the Susquehanna River. After the flood, the hospital used funds from FEMA and New York State to build a new floodwall. The floodwall was designed to protect the hospital from future floodwaters. In 2011, Tropical Storm Lee hit the community. This time, the floodwall protected the hospital. The hospital stayed open and avoided major storm damage.

A floodwall protects Lourdes Hospital in New York from flood waters. The wall was built with funds from FEMA and New York State.

After the devastation of Hurricane Katrina in New Orleans, FEMA has paid almost $2 billion to help the state of Louisiana pay for flood prevention projects.

New flood control systems protect the city of New Orleans.

Careers with FEMA

It takes many people working together to prepare for and respond to a disaster. Some employees have full time jobs with FEMA. Others are hired for temporary jobs when a disaster strikes. FEMA employees arrive after state and local first responders. They interview disaster victims and **assess** damage. They organize rescue missions. They provide support during and after a disaster. FEMA specialists include engineers, architects, teachers, and emergency managers. FEMA also employs geologists and environmental scientists who study how to lower the risk of a natural disaster. To learn more look up: http://**www.fema.gov/careers**

When a fierce flood, hurricane, tornado, or blizzard strikes, many people can be injured or killed. Millions of dollars of property may be destroyed or damaged. A deadly tornado can destroy an entire neighborhood in a few minutes. A devastating hurricane can leave people without electricity, water, or heat for days or weeks at a time. In a disaster, people may not be able to travel because roads are damaged and bridges are washed out.

Community agencies partner with FEMA to aid in disaster recovery.

When disaster hits, FEMA employees work with local and state governments to get help to the people who need it. They help set up shelters for people who cannot stay at their homes. They hand out food, water, clothes, and blankets. When people are hurt, FEMA employees set up medical stations so doctors and nurses can treat the injured. They assist emergency teams that search for survivors, clear wreckage, and repair power and communications systems.

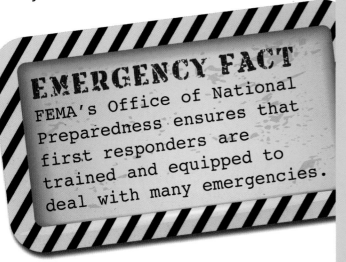

EMERGENCY FACT
FEMA's Office of National Preparedness ensures that first responders are trained and equipped to deal with many emergencies.

FEMA Corps

Created in 2012, FEMA Corps is a team of young Americans ages 18–24 who have volunteered to serve during disasters. A unit in AmeriCorps' National Civilian Community Corps, FEMA Corps members are devoted exclusively to disaster response and recovery. After being trained in emergency response, the unit's 1,600 members work with disaster survivors, man disaster recovery centers, help citizens prepare for disaster, and perform other critical tasks. Each member serves for a 10-month term, with the ability to serve for a second term. When they complete their service, members are prepared for future careers in emergency management and other related fields.

In 2012, Hurricane Sandy devastated the northeast United States. More than one hundred people died. Thousands of homes flooded. Millions of people lost electrical power.

Yet even before the storm hit, FEMA was preparing. They worked with local and state agencies to prepare an emergency response plan.

Officials from FEMA and the Department of Homeland Security meet with President Barack Obama at the White House to prepare for Hurricane Sandy.

Hurricane Sandy was the most destructive hurricane of the 2012 Atlantic hurricane season.

The National Guard distributes food and water at a local Disaster Recovery Center after Hurricane Sandy.

FEMA employees brought food, water, and equipment into New Jersey to be ready once the storm passed. FEMA teams were on site, working alongside local agencies.

Within 48 hours of the storm hitting, 1,200 FEMA employees were in the field. Some went door to door in affected neighborhoods. Others worked at supply bases providing meals and water. Still others helped people find temporary housing. FEMA also opened disaster recovery centers to help people affected by the storm.

After a disaster, FEMA helps people recover and rebuild their lives. Often this recovery work starts very soon after the disaster. Sometimes, it can last for years.

At FEMA's disaster recovery stations, people get information about services and grants to help them repair their homes and find housing. FEMA officials can also help people apply for loans and grants to reopen businesses and farms. People who have lost jobs because of the disaster can apply for money to pay for living expenses.

FEMA workers answer questions about services and assistance at a Disaster Recovery Center.

FEMA also provides other types of disaster assistance. In a disaster, family members may become separated and have no way to contact each other. FEMA runs a family registry system that helps family members find each other. FEMA officials even assist local groups in finding missing pets. FEMA offers crisis counseling to people who are scared or have suffered a great loss.

Animal Resource Centers reunite owners with lost pets. Centers also supply pet food, supplies, and medical attention after an emergency.

FEMA is helping to design and build stronger, safer homes.

After Hurricane Sandy in 2012, FEMA officials **coordinated** the efforts of national, state, and local groups. One year later, FEMA had made more than $1.4 billion in payments to more than 182,000 survivors. FEMA also approved more than $3.2 billion for emergency work, **debris** removal, and **infrastructure** repair and replacement.

Before, during, and after a disaster, FEMA will be there to help people in the United States.

TIMELINE

1803:
Federal government helps the residents of a New Hampshire town after a fire.

1974:
Congress passes the Disaster Relief Act.

1930s:
The government begins to plan how to prevent and help during disasters.

1979:
President Jimmy Carter creates FEMA.

1989:
FEMA coordinates the federal response to the Loma Prieta Earthquake in California.

2003:
FEMA becomes part of the Department of Homeland Security.

2001:
FEMA responds when terrorists strike the United States on September 11.

2012:
Hurricane Sandy devastates the Northeast. FEMA coordinates disaster relief services.

GLOSSARY

agency (AY-juhn-see): an office or a business that provides a service to the public

assess (uh-SESS): to judge how bad a disaster is and how much damage it caused

civil defense (SIV-il di-FENZ): responding to an attack or natural disaster with rescue efforts

communications systems (kuh-MYOO-nuh-kay-shuhn SISS-tuhmz): network of phone lines, computers, faxes, and other equipment that allows people to talk to each other and share information

coordinated (koh-OR-duh-nated): organized activities or people that all work together

counseling (KOUN-suhl-ing): helping people deal with their losses and how their lives change after a disaster

debris (duh-BREE): the scattered pieces of something that has been destroyed

evacuated (i-VAK-yoo-ate-id): removed from a place that is dangerous to a place that is safe

federal (FED-ur-uhl): relating to the national government

first responders (FURST ruh-SPON-durz): emergency medical workers who are the first people to arrive at a disaster or emergency

floodplains (FLUHD-planez): low, flat land that sometimes floods

infrastructure (IN-fruh-struhk-cher): the basic systems of a community, such as roads, buildings, and power plants

mitigation (mit-i-GEY-shun): trying to prevent disaster damage by taking steps to make land and buildings safe

oversees: (OH-vur-seez): supervises a person or activity

property (PROP-ur-tee): something that is owned, like a house or land

simulating (sim-yuh-LAY-ting): pretending

toxic (TOK-sik): poisonous

INDEX

SHOW WHAT YOU KNOW

1. Why was FEMA founded?
2. How does FEMA help before a disaster strikes?
3. What is FEMA's role during a natural disaster?
4. What types of man-made disasters could affect Americans?
5. How did FEMA help after Hurricane Sandy?

WEBSITES TO VISIT

www.dhs.gov
www.fema.gov
www.ready.gov/kids

31

About the Author

Carla Mooney has written many books for children and young adults. She lives in Pennsylvania with her husband and three children. She enjoys learning about U.S. history and reading stories of everyday heroes protecting America.

Meet The Author!
www.meetREMauthors.com

www.rourkeeducationalmedia.com

PHOTO CREDITS: Cover Photo by David Fine / FEMA; Page 4-5 © Benjamin Simeneta; Page 6 Norman Lenburg/FEMA, Page 7 George Armstrong/FEMA; Page 8a Photo by Shannon Arledge/FEMA , Page 9 Michael Rieger/FEMA; Pages 10-12 © NOAA; Page 13 courtesy os U.S. government; Page 14 photo by Master Sgt. Mark C. Olsen/U.S. Air Force/New Jersey National Guard; Page 15 flood photo © NOAA; Page 16-17 © Dan Schreiber, Page 16 inset Photo by Sharon Karr/FEMA; Page 18 Photo by FEMA News, Page 19 Jacinta Quesada/FEMA Page 20 FEMA News; Page 22 Weather photo courtesy of NASA, situation room courtesy U.S. government, Page 23 Jocelyn Augustino/FEMA; Page 24 FEMA Photo by Win Henderson, Page 25 K.C.Wilsey/FEMA; Page 26-27 Photo by Ralph Simcox, Inset photo Andrea Booher/FEMA; Page 29 Michael Rieger/ FEMA News Photo

Edited by: Jill Sherman

Designed and Produced by: Nicola Stratford   www.nicolastratford.com

Library of Congress Cataloging-in-Publication Data

Mooney. Carla.
  FEMA: Prepare, Respond, and Recover / Carla Mooney
  p. cm. -- (Emergency Response)
  ISBN 978-1-62717-656-9 (hard cover) (alk. paper)
  ISBN 978-1-62717-778-8 (soft cover)
  ISBN 978-1-62717-897-6 (e-book)
 Library of Congress Control Number: 2014934249

Rourke Educational Media
Printed in the United States of America,
North Mankato, Minnesota

Also Available as:
ROURKE'S
e-Books